SEEKING *Identities*

PARUL KAPOOR

INDIA • SINGAPORE • MALAYSIA

Copyright © Parul Kapoor 2024
All Rights Reserved.

ISBN 979-8-89446-673-6

| ॐ Om Namah Shivay ॐ |

*To Lord Shiva, who has constantly illuminated my path,
allowing me to seek and rise.*

To my parents, for bestowing upon me a great education.

To my family, for their unwavering support and motivation.

Contents

SEEKING LOVE AND RELATIONSHIPS

SEEKING RESPONSIBILITIES

Prologue

This poetry book is an exploration on human nature, shedding light on our tendency to cling to certain identities while relinquishing others. Often, the identities we strive to maintain are not necessarily those that authentically resonate with our inner selves; rather, they are frequently shaped by external influences and societal expectations.

In our pursuit of the elusive perfect identity, we stumble upon imperfect ones along the way. We adopt these identities as vehicles for self-exploration, peeling back the layers to uncover what lies within. With each layer we add, older identities may fade into the inner realms, like the graves which got buried under the weight of heavy stones, waiting to be unearthed through introspection. These layers of identity serve as the fabric of our transformative journey—a journey that unfolds unexpectedly yet is deeply lived and experienced.

Through this collection of poetry, I invite you to delve into the complex tapestry of identities we continually *seek* -- as individuals, as partners in love, as parents, and at times, in our quest for solace.

Come, join me in this poetic voyage of self-discovery and introspection through SEEKING.

If you enjoy a poem or want to share excerpts from it, use the hashtag #seekingidentities when tagging.

– **Parul Kapoor**
(A seeker for lifetime)

Seeking Identity

Identity

/aɪˈdɛntɪti/

the state or fact of remaining the same one or ones, as under varying aspects or conditions

---

"Identity is a prison you can never escape, but the way to redeem your past is not to run from it, but to try to understand it, and use it as a foundation to grow."

– Jay-Z

Certain identities act as mere placeholders. They don't linger, but upon departure, they leave indelible marks. These imprints may take the form of scars, wounds, cloaks, or occasionally medals that we wear tirelessly, yearning for their healing touch. They possess the power to alter the very essence of our souls permanently. While they may not always be visible, they emerge repeatedly through the crevices etched within our souls, striking us at just the right moment, rousing us from our deepest slumbers, signalling that the time for metamorphosis has arrived.

We live to seek
Those untold truths
Which shape our poetic souls
Or dig our artistic graves maybe
We seek to explore the unknowns
and at times the known
to fall into those dark ravines
where the thin beam of light
takes us deep within
to the innermost corners
where tales from our past perch
where tales from our future manifest in a churning pot
where our folklores are being sung by the flames of hope
where the memories are frozen
from the volcanic eruptions to turn blue-black
where the guilt is overtaken by turmoil brewing inside
where happiness shines through after a grey downpour
where all is calm when seen from a naked eye
but a ferocious whirlpool of emotions pirouettes within
quivering the empty voids of our soul
to embark us on a journey of seeking

– Seeking within

My unacknowledged identity
Craves for meagre recognition
To nourish its parched soul
Which awaits to settle
From the unending journey
Traversing the expansive multiverses
With no sense of direction, and no guiding light
It meanders the craters of uncertainty
and rocks of ignorance
It bumps into strangers
Who scorn its existence
And impart it with misnomers
Casually applauding the efforts
Which took a lifetime to become
Rarely celebrating its achievements
My identity wades through
the marshy wetlands which sink beneath
And pull it into the immeasurable abyss
Meanwhile the world celebrates
crowning of the privileged
and my unacknowledged identity
watches as a mute spectator

– The unacknowledged identity

My growth resembled
The tiny seed
Seeking to break open
Or explode maybe
But the weight of soil
Suffocated me
Like the world was saying
Why grow when you can wane away
While I longed to grow
Like the lanky sunflower in the fields
Which arced towards the sun
Who brought it to life
I wish I had such a sun
Which would shine upon me
And bestow its warmth
For me to sprout or explode maybe

– Growth

Growth is not an individual process but a collective one. It is a manifestation of our surroundings our observations and experiences bundled into a surprise package which needs to be carefully unpacked layer by layer

– Layers of growth

My piecemeal identity

Forages for a name, to fit its nomadic soul

It tries various outfits

Some are fit, some are misfit

But it does not seek the fit

Instead it seeks respect, pride and contentment

as the adorned attire

It seeks to reflect to the world

it's glorious hard work and the self-taught skills

Which make it proud inside

But fails to impress outside

As the world does not fathom perfection

Rather embraces mediocrity

screaming of attention and self-loathing

Which my piecemeal identity shrugs off

As it prefers to stay put

But refuses to wear the fictitious shroud

– The fictitious attire

The world split my soul into two

like the Janus coin

A double face

Engraved forever

Appearing flawless at the top

but running with fractured lines deep inside

the two faces reflecting my broken persona

switching sides to manoeuvre

the Janus-faced world.

My twin sides reflect --

A Soul: scarred yet unhurt

Form: dislocated yet structured

Appearance: Messy yet polished

Demeanour: Burnt yet calm

Both images belong to me

But I am none

I am just performing

With a Janus-face mask

– Janus faced

The unfamiliar image in the mirror

bore an unknown shade

It exuded calm

So unlike me

Frightened I stepped back

While the image smiled

Scrupulously I took puny steps

And touched the mirror

to feel the forbidden pleasures

It sprinkled me with some intrepidity

To fight my intrinsic demons

It showered some rationality onto

To balance my jittery mind

It tickled me with a hint of humour

To enliven my mundane persona

It saturated me with serenity

To tranquilise my healing soul

– The unknown shade

The place looked familiar
But felt oddly strange
I called it the second home
But was never warm enough

Despite the quietness
Existed a silent storm
Of slanderous rumours
And friendly betrayals
Of defiant attitudes
And antagonist breezes

My growing presence was discussed
at coffee breaks, gossip sessions
at official meetings
even beyond work hours
at times spilling into whatsapp messages

Endeavours were made
to surveil my life
which was an open book anyways
where chapters existed randomly
where quotes appeared naturally

where nothing was complete

where everything was scattered

like the pile of office papers

which had been rummaged for evidence

I stayed longer than I should have

Hoping for the warmth to seep in someday

Through the structural cracks

Of the place I called

My second home

Which never felt warm enough

– The cold 'second' home

A familiar whiff hovers
As I enter through the doors
The dishevelled pantry oozes the aroma of burnt milk
Overflowing on the ancient hotplate
aged and enriched with layers of murky tea
waiting to be poured into cheap white bone china mugs
engraved with the stately seal

The stale draught from the heavy air conditioning
Mixed with the fragrance of budgeted air fresheners
a shady concoction emerges
To welcome the privileged

'Clack-clack' – the sound of leather boots
Reverberate the swanky corridors
Which have seen visionaries walk through
to the doors which say
'OFFICIALS ONLY, DO NOT ENTER'

The leader enters and we all rise
Like the ministers do when the king walks in
The ceremony commences with relaxed conversations
Spanning the length and breadth of the globe
Subtly hinting their bustling schedules and packed itineraries

While I admire the distinguished and varying tones

which give away hints of sovereignty

The stale air in the room

Feels stuffed and overpowering

From the hidden glances

Which inspect my identity

and label it as an outlander

but ask me to follow the herd

– Aroma of the distinguished

Recipe to create *crushed-identity* soda:

1. Take a vulnerable soul
2. Pour a spoonful of possessiveness concentrate
3. Stir with mindful sarcasm
4. Drizzle with sweet bitterness
5. Sprinkle a pinch of constant denial
6. Garnish with zests of exotic sham

Serve chilled!

Enjoy

– The identity drink

My bravest self, if I may tell you

Would be Brave!

Brave enough to dance and twirl around

As I possess four left feet

Brave enough to sing melodious songs

As I pity the audience in the street

Brave enough to stand tall in the crowd

As I am just little above five feet

Brave enough to talk out loud

As I am often asked to repeat

Brave enough to disturb someone

As I rarely poke and stay aloof

Brave enough to love the rain

As I so wish the rain was waterproof

Brave enough to act child-like

As I always try and comfort the rest

Brave enough to climb the mountain

As there are thousand things on my quest

– If I was my bravest self

I get ready to leave

But forget to put on the blush of courage

Left in a haste

And landed at the party feeling underdressed

Looked around to spot courage

walking towards me and say

'Are you new here?'

I say 'I don't think I belong, but I want to settle'

The air of confidence in the room makes me feel naked

I rush to put on the mascara of self-doubt

which I always carry

to hide my homegrown flaws

then hit the bar and ask for a virgin mojito

The bartender says 'I don't serve unadulterated'

I gulp the vodka shot offered instead

And a deadly concoction of anxiety

mixed with hatred hit me

I borrow some courage from the room

and arrive at the dance floor to realise,

everyone is naked,

I feel settled now

– The naked party

Slow down, pause

Be kind and gentle to yourself

Do not rush

it would all be fine one day

Words and phrases which I long to fill in my world of fantasies

Move on..

Ignore..

Do not think, just act as told..

You are being unreasonable now..

Words and phrases which adorn my world of realism

– Realism

The sun peeked through the slit in the clouds

Like a new bride looks through her long-drawn veil

It changed positions to shine through perfectly

Like the new bride changes her name to gain identity

It lightened its glare to match the soothing clouds

Like the new bride tries to blend into the crowd

Little did the sun know the shift would be seen as submission

And its identity would be overtaken

Like the new bride is told to draw a veil

to hide her melancholic tales

– The bride like sun

Soaked in celebrations, immersed in pride

The city bedecked like a new bride

It smiles coyly to welcome the guests

Since few days she had no rest

Artists examine her scarred looks

Debate within she might need more than hooks

Heal the scar, put some foundation

Smear the walls with accolades of the nation

Line the avenues with exotic varieties

The guest shall know we have a modern society

Put billboards and hide pleats of poverty

Sweep the roads to dust shades of anxiety

Scatter some sculptures here and there

It would distract from the messy public squares

Add large fountains to soothe the heat

When all done Let's put up a tweet (X)

Let the citizens dream and capture

Drown them in the spirit– *one earth, one family, one future*

Roll out the red carpet, guests would be here soon

Ask the bride to draw the veil and wait for the groom

– The bedecked city
(an ode to the city before G20 summit)

The wedding is over

The carpets are rolled

The guests have flown back

With memories warm and cold

The city returns to its usual cacophony

The chatter, the chaos, the daily monotony

The groom happily rests on the bed of accolades

While the bride's makeup slowly begins to fade

The torn billboards reveal the inner crust

Scattered, littered, smeared with dust

The homeless are back to their heavenly shacks

The guests didn't get a whiff of the systematic cracks

The city glows in its timeless glory

The ruins of the monuments whisper an enchanted story

The river reeks of industrial sludge

But we worship it still without prejudge

This is the bride (city) which was bedecked last night

With fairy lights glistening the mandap

with a hue deep & bright

But today it sings a melancholic song

While weeping silently like a bride forgotten for aeons.

– The lost glory
(an ode to the city after G20 summit)

Seeking Solace

solace

/sol-is/

comfort in sorrow, misfortune, or trouble; alleviation of distress or discomfort.

"I firmly believe that nature brings solace in all troubles"

— Anne Frank

I was seeking for darkness, when I had energy of *SUNLIGHT* around

I was seeking for pale, when I had the lustre of *FLOWERS* around

I was seeking for silence, when I had chirping of *BIRDS* around

I was seeking for madness, when I had the *CALMNESS* of sea around

I was seeking for innocence, when I had the *MISCHIEVOUSNESS* of the squirrels around

I was seeking for bruises, when I had the healing from *SPRINGS* around

I chose nature's embrace over darkness, and now I have *LIFE* around

We humans are merely a speck of dust in this world who carry loads of ego and remain self - centred to fulfil our desires and ambitions. Only if we shed this fictitious skin and live our lives with a little humility and empathy we might start becoming significant in this lifetime

– Fictitious skin

We have got entangled in our own web where we work hard to seek the time and money which would bring us Joy, but when we want to enjoy that Joy we don't as our definition has changed while we were chasing it

– The web of joy

He guides us in those days

While we wander directionless, aimless

He paves the path which lay invisible to our naked eyes.

The path which always existed

But was invisible to our sub-consciousness

we constantly seek but never ask - Why we seek?

The power, the name

The lust, the fame

Are these the only ingredients to survive

Isn't it the inner calling

Isn't it the inner child

Isn't it the curiosity

Isn't it the deep desire

He teaches us to be patient

When the storm hits us inside

And asks us to listen to the sound of the waves

Crashing against the thin layered walls of our hollow souls

Which only listen to the mind and heart

And not the sub-conscious which does not only listen

But breathes life as well

He asks us to let the waves carry the power within

That emanated from his mighty tresses

He asks us to imbibe the calmness and fierceness together

And chose them when the time comes

He asks us to believe in ourselves

As he has believed in us till immortality hits us

For we seek Him, when we are lost

While he has always been inside paving that path

Which lay invisible as we were busy seeking

The path which never existed

– Seeking HIM

The naked autumn trees

Have shed their leaves

And revealed layers

With patterns of hidden scars

like prints etched

in its dormant memories

Losing color as seasons transition

Stinging each time.

The chilled winds pass by

The trees wait mercilessly for the winters

To stab open old wounds

Like someone dug open a grave

that had been rustling in the past

As someone didn't bury it properly

And left petty gaps

In haste of time

Without bothering about the soul

Which lay inside and waited

for the winters to pass by

Let the spring come in

So that the rays of sunshine

Fall upon its dusty spirit

And wipe clean the wounds

Which had been let open

In the last summer

While the earth burned like ashes

And the parched soil

Left the seed craving for the monsoon

To quench its thirst and let it explode

With the thrust of water which swelled the rivers

waited for the torrential rains to stop

So that they could slow down a bit

And save the trees which had

perished under its fierceness

Who craved for the autumn instead

So that they could at least stay still

Even if they felt naked

In the autumn days.

– The bruised seasons

Be a volcano

But don't burn within

Ooze out the lava and release the grief

That stuck to the bottom of your soul for so long

Show to the world your mighty prowess

Your desire to grow within

like roots of the banyan tree

Be a volcano outside

But be a waterfall inside

Filling your soul with sulphurous waters

Nourishing the layers which got burnt

by the embers thrown at by the world

Be a volcano

to light up the dark night like the stars do

and not for self-destruction

save the lava for a greater purpose

as the world does not even deserve it's fierceness

– Volcano

How do I know, what lies within me

Fear, love, courage or pain?

My scattered thoughts create a whirlpool

Which look like tangents, angles,

intersecting lines and rays co-existing

To create a confused geometric shape called life.

I look for answers around

In the sky, trees, rivers and oceans

I stop people and ask,

if they have key to my investigation

Who fail to even comprehend

Just when I hear a voice which whispers

"What you look for, lies within

You are the fire, you are the earth,

you are the sky, you are the oceans

Come, knock on the door of your inner spirit

And enter the gateway which says,

'Welcome to the world of seeking"

– Discovery

The journey of dreams can manifest into reality when it is dolloped with limitless and wild passion No luck, fortune or serendipity can strike us, if we do not crave for a soulful journey

– Soulful journey

The stillness after rains paint a dreamy scene

While we wait to see reflections from the past

They tell the tales of our quixotic selves

While we long for our broken souls to awaken

The freshly washed leaves bring faithful promises

While we hold on to forgotten moments

The crispness of the still wet air ushers in modern romance

While we long to dance barefoot to the tunes of unsung songs

The fragrance of the Earth invites us to liberate ourselves

While we long to travel to forbidden paths

The grey-blue skies send us signals to fly

While we seek to bask in the warmth of the sun

Suddenly the wind blows over the reflections from the past

And leave us with memories which are washed away with the
rains.

– Reflections from stillness

Her presence bought a calm

Accompanied by some hope of resuscitation

She patiently let me wail

Then calmly held my tremored hands

While I poured my darkest memories

To fill the seas of sorrow

She gently caressed my delicate soul

Like a mother does to her new born

She surrendered her precious time

To hear my tales of agony

She nurtured me with a dose of hug and embrace

And asked me to be kind to myself

Her touch finally bought silence to the chaos

Which was shattering my peaceful soul

I embraced her like a new born embraces mother's flesh

As she is mother nature who accepted me as I am.

– The healing touch

The morning light falls on the dewy leaves
And whisper a secret into their ears
The wind flows swiftly through the woods
And creates a rustling sound
The birds sit atop the tall pine trees
And sing melodious tunes to them
The butterflies meander through the grass
And enliven the quiet zen looking garden
The honey bees cluster together in a swarm
And start their morning chores
This is how nature wakes up every day
-- chirpy, undisturbed and unperturbed
To paint a beautiful scenery called
'a bountiful day in the life of woods'

– Life in woods

The falling of the leaves onto the streets

Waiting to be snuggled into a pile

Reminds of life coming to a full circle

Which tells us

nothing is permanent, nothing is static

But what remains the same is the bountiful nature

Which never ceases to gift us with new life every day

No matter we care, no matter we don't

It would close the circle and bestow us with a fresh new start

With rays of sun falling onto the scattered leaves

Waiting to be snuggled into a pile

To close the nature's circle.

– Nature's circle

Nature, oh beautiful creature
I longed to meet you
And when I did, I was mesmerised
By your divine creations
Which kept pulling me back into your laps
Where I felt comfort and solace

The forests you created
Are like heaven on earth
Peaceful and majestic
Calm and royal
I often come here for wild walks
Where I get lost within its mightiness

The rivers you brew
Are full of life
Slow and intense
Quiet and rapid
I often sit by them to listen over
Under a full moon night

The oceans you fill
Are giant reservoirs

Vast and deep

Soothing and furious

I often hit them for a swim

When I feel like meditating

Nature, Oh beautiful creature

I met you at the rivers , forests and seas

Where I immersed in your beauty

Which was grander than any being

And I decided to stay back forever

To never come out of this beautiful dream

– Nature's rendezvous

Seeking Light

light

/laɪt/

noun - a condition of spiritual awareness; divine illumination

---

"There is always light. If only we're brave enough to see it. If only we're brave enough to be it."

— *Amanda Gorman*

Let's not disdain darkness, for it imparts profound life lessons. It guides us to unexplored realms, preparing us to confront the demons we encounter on the path to growth, success, and renewal. Darkness teaches us to welcome silence and heed our inner voices. It resembles meditation, while becoming the gateway to our subconscious, enabling us to ready ourselves for the unveiling of new opportunities.

Instead, let us take darkness as a force which urges us to listen to our mind, body and soul. A conversation which we never struck as we were engaged or aloof, as we were hypnotised or spooked.

So much to think, so much to absorb

So much that I don't know where to pause

The unstoppable chatter, the relentless banter

The unthinkable thoughts that behave like a monster

I keep procrastinating, I keep hallucinating

I keep messing up only to fall into the trap of repeating

All this happens while I live inside a dream

Inside the dream I fall and I scream,

I then wake up to watch the merciless reality

Where my dreams and aspirations are crushed with cruelty

Scared to accept the truthful lie

I once again close my eyes

I watch my world crumble under the domino effect

I wish I knew how to disconnect

Reality is not for my scarred and torn soul

My life feels like a fish trapped in a waterless bowl

– Relentless chatter

Our minds are mostly chaotic like that wardrobe which has been mercilessly dumped with random clothes in the hope that they would someday be worn and celebrated. Some clothes are worn, but some stay hanged with the bill intact forgotten but still occupying space in the cluttered wardrobe.

– The cluttered wardrobe

Scattered pieces of puzzled thoughts,

Strewn around my cluttered mind

Paint a chaotic scene,

Far from a life defined

Directionless and aimless I wander,

In search of a guiding light

Unable to decide the next move,

I suddenly stumble upon something bright

Navigating my way through the tunnel,

I brave my way amidst the dark

Only to find at the end,

That the light was just a far-away spark

– Light at end of the tunnel

I laid still in the darkness and searched for solace.

when memories flashing from the forlorn past

made me stop to gaze.

The images were a part of the tattered reel,

Waiting to be seen, heard and unveiled

Some looked dark

Some looked blurred

Some looked cold

Some looked stirred

Some looked dirty

some looked numb

some looked mysterious

some looked succumbed

But none was clear

The solace was gone, the mind was flooded

The darkness had returned, the moon turned bloodied

I struggled to open the eyes, and come back to the darkness

while the memories pulled me back with a sting of sharpness

– Memories from the past

Celebrating small victories would be far more fulfilling than crying over lost chances knowing that the victory was always yours and the lost chance never belonged.

– Victories

Life these days is edgy

While the days are filled with tasks I yearn for

The mind in its lonely state is not calm

It seeks to find those answers

Which have no definite value or logic

They just have a word which guides them –'*destiny*'

This word comes with disagreements

It does not address discussions about

love, attachment and connections

It only discusses fate which remains to be a '*no control zone*'

Where decisions are not discussed, but are taken

Dictated by our past sins

and sometimes by the *Moirai* (sisters)

Who do not ask what we want,

but declare that we shall

No matter we work hard, struggle or wither

Our story has been authored

Which cannot be changed but only lived

As we are the custodians and not the creators

And shall take care of this life

Which has been illustrated by the *Moirai* (sisters)

– Moirai

The rebel in me, fights an invisible battle

    With demons who pledge no harm

    With noises which never scream

    With illusions which never tempt

    With darkness that never engulfs

    With strangers that never disturb

The rebel in me, fights a conspicuous battle

    With words which were never spoken but heard

    With tasks which were never finished, but surrendered

    With visions which were never seen, but dreamt

    With deadlines which were never set, but felt

    With friends which never met, but hurt

    With myself who is a rebel, but never pretends

– The delusional rebel

Life keeps bringing us back to the prompts that are circling us so that we catch hold of them to find more answers and connect the scattered dots like the patterns of constellations which hold promises and hopes of future

– Prompts

I walk barefoot one last time to feel my skin

But get scared to part ways

as I might be committing a sin

But it's time to move on

As it's the beginning of a new dawn

I begin to shed the heavy layers tying me

Full of insecurities, self-doubt and vulnerability

I now prepare to don my new armour

Loaded with weapons which make me a charmer

The rays of the sun fall lightly on the ground

They touch my skin and heal my wounds

I embrace the new layers, welcome with open arms

remembering my holy God, I chant with folded palms

– Shedding old layers

Days

Turning into nights

Long, hopeless nights

And then again long days

Filling our lives with sorrows and some hope

Hope of recovery

Hope of gratitude and existence

Hope that someday it would be sunshine

Which would heal our scars

who's blood has turned toxic

So toxic

That it's killing us inside

– Toxic days

Seeking Love and Relationships

/lʌv/

Love is a strong liking for something, or a belief that it is important.

Relationships can be intricate, given the expectations intertwined with them.

Expectation of love in return

Expectation of being truthful

Expectation of loving unconditionally

Expectation of not asking but telling

Expectation of being present when the other was not

Expectation of running chores alone when it is a shared gig

In the pursuit of fixing the discipline, we frequently overlook their true essence

And thus we lose either ourselves or our loved ones

In the hustle of perfecting our relationships

As humans we are constantly investing in material friendships, superficial and loose relationships to conceal the buried emotions and despair. We often prefer to ignore the falsities and rather welcome the mediocrities which keep us entertained for brief moments of time but later throw us back into our complicated existences.

– Loose threads

I feel scared to reveal my subtle sentiments

while my partner pours their hearts out

I become a recluse upon receiving undue attention

While my partner craves for nuggets of flirty comments

I feel creepy in the embrace of condensed admiration

While my partner awaits a bucketful of praises

I feel cranky when I am asked

to greet the dawn with a peck on the cheek

while my partner longs for

mushy mornings between the naked sheets

I stand cold to curated gifts and thoughtful wishes

While my partner enjoys a mixed bag of emotions

I turn sheepish when he asks me to hold hands in public

While my partner yearns for intimate jacuzzi baths

I feel anorexic on romantic dates;

candlelight dinners make me nauseated

While my partner covets the buffet of a happy couple

Entry No. 124 of 510

Excerpts from my long list of confessions

Which I wrote to myself

– Confessions of an awkward lover

Their eyes met at the junction

Bustling with vendors

selling fragrance called love

Calling names from above

Everything changed that moment

Nothing was same,

Not even their name

A fire ignited like a blast

A tornado bringing back memories from the past

A subtle nod confirmed the faith

A hidden smile caressed the face

A silent prayer chanted within

A desire to talk but knew it was sin

They knew they could never unite

But found each other, what a respite!

One last wish, one last song

Their love story lasted for aeons

– The lost love

I walked the path beside you

In the hope of becoming your companion

Waiting to be welcomed by

The bouquet of acceptance

Instead I was adorned with

The baggage of responsibilities

I embraced the garland of chores

And wore it over my bridal dress

And was showered with rituals

of religion and culture

I soaked my soul in hues of red to imbibe the verses

And was judged for the easy acceptance

I shut my senses to my inner circle

And was declared as anti-social

I trusted you to build me a castle

But you chose an embellished cage instead

– Welcome to the new home

Trust me, he said

I closed my eyes and took a deep breath

While his words echoing my senses

Take a step forward, bend your knees and get ready

A gush of wind, hit my face

Like a rock thrown from far away

I yearned to pull back to my comfortable bed

And abandon the gruesome trust test.

I turned back to him and looked into his mighty eyes

Which smiled and said – '*don't worry, trust me*'

Tucking my chest in to block the synthetic smell

From churning the acid in my gut

I took one last deep breath

And chanted my holy prayers

Dive. A whistle.

I jumped into and hit the blue bottom

My body felt the burning sensation

As the water entered my lungs

While the hazy figure stood above

With the same friendly smile

chanting the words -- '*don't worry, trust me*'

– Trust issues

The hue of my love isn't red anymore

It's a shade darker than that drop of blood

Which felt like tears on my blemished face

burning the scars which were left behind —

Untreated and unkind

I receded my love, withdrew my emotions

Announcing the demise of my love for strangers

Stranger who is anyone but me

Stranger who cannot be me

As my frail heart did not wish more blemishes

Which could shatter my dead but craving soul

Craving for a lover

Who never asked but loved

Who never betrayed only stayed

A lover who coloured me the shade of red

Which was the new shade of love

– Hue of love

I wish my love was as deep as yours

Deep enough to touch someone's heart when they are not grieving

Deep enough to tell them they are loved when they are not seeking

Deep enough to comfort them when they are not weeping

Deep enough to listen when no one is speaking

Deep enough to be just around when they wish to be alone

I wish my love was as deep as yours, I wish it was not unknown.

– Desires in love

Some of us have old friends as part of the circle some add new at later stages in life but the central idea remains the same. As long as it provides us the comfort and the positivity that we yearn for it's worth being a part of that circle.I don't even mind if today my inner circle is just a dot.

– The inner circle

Seeking Responsibilities

/ri-spon-suh-bil-i-tee/

the state or fact of being responsible, answerable, or accountable for something within one's power, control, or management

---

"You become responsible, forever, for what you have tamed."

— Antoine de Saint-Exupéry, The Little Prince

Responsibilities is indeed a heavy word, laden with a spectrum of emotions.

We embark on the path of responsibility in distinct manners – either by choice, chance or force

When we are responsible by choice, we enjoy the journey. For instance, being a parent by choice would be a joyous experience as one looks forward to spending time with their children and finds meaningful ways to do so.

However, when we are responsible by chance, we begin to prepare for the challenges and learn our ways through; whereas when we are made to be responsible by force, then it becomes a struggle.

That is where the real test begins – whether to chose joy over struggle or struggle enough to attain joy.

Parenting is a rough terrain and the best part is that no one tells it beforehand. We all learn from our experiences but at the end of the day what matters is the fact that our kids need us emotionally and vice-versa. There maybe times when we are not physically around but a parent is always hovering around the child in invisible ways as we need to be sure that our little creations are safe, sound and ever-evolving.

– Parenting

Maybe its okay to cry at times

To vent out

To say its not okay to be asked to be okay

To let others know every day is not a happy day

To shrug people off and go back

into your snuggled, comfortable cocoons

Where its your loneliness giving you company

To make you happy like no one does

To finally dream that dream

which got faded and buried away in the past

under the burden of responsibilities

like that pile of laundry

which refuses to cease

Lets try to breathe free at times

Lets try to to live life like a child does

As why become a sad adult

when you can be a happy child

– Breathing responsibilities

She wades through the living room
On a cold Sunday morning
When her loved ones are snoozing comfortably
under their warm overdrawn cloaks
She gathers their scattered possessions
Which they left behind on their way to the dens
which were strewn like shells
that lay on the deserted shore
She felt like the ocean waves
which brought the shells back home
so that the loved ones could make garlands of laughter
and adorn them while heading out for social interactions
She caresses the shells as if they were her offspring
who have outgrown the rituals of hugs, cuddles and kisses
And now seek for solitude in aloofness
She tiptoes her way through the narrow labyrinth of corridors
into an area that bears the announcement
"you are entering a personal den,

enter at your own risk"
Slowly sneaking like a thief does upon robbery
feeling like perpetrating a deadly sin
she crawls into the den to settle the possessions

while assuring her cubs do not arouse from deep slumbers
she pauses to watch them snooze peacefully
while hesitating to hug, cuddle and kiss them
and embraces the shells instead
bestowing the fragrance of the outgrown offsprings

– The outgrown offsprings

I sprint over a hurdle to reach the flame

dancing on one toe I ace this game

I twirl and catch the specks of dust

remove the cobwebs, this is my list of wanderlust

The pile of clothes and the stacks of dominos

they are ready to crumble, oh catch them while I strike a pose!

The scattered books resemble volcano rocks

careful honey, the floor is lava — jump onto that box!

The dishes are greasy, laden with citrus

don't worry let me don the hat of the mighty dish-mistress

The floor is stained from the wine last night

Oh, I spilled it accidently, please don't mind

The laundry is done I need to put them away

these maids don't come on time I should fire them today

The pasta water has boiled, I must simmer it down

I don't like the color of the sauce, this golden brown

The school assignment is top on my to-do list

You should check that new tutor out, Oh I insist!

These unending, everyday chores

turn me into a meticulous juggler

Oh, but don't be afraid I am no smuggler

What I do crave for although is a life

full of laughter, joy and some unadulterated fun

For this life is given to us only once!

– The parenting dance

I assemble fragments of the final attire
Like bits of a 1000-piece jigsaw puzzle
A pile of DIY books strewn around
I emerge victorious from the rubble
The hat, the cape,
the broom, the snake,
Caress me like my jewellery
I wear the tiara proudly on my head
Pretending to play devilry
I act like a queen,
I act like a warrior
I act like the superhero,
but finally become the courtier
I then put on some makeup in shades of ivory
To hide my hideous role
Roll on expensive mascara and blush
to disguise my facial mole
the audience is waiting eagerly,
but I struggle to memorise the chants
Soon to wake up with a jerk
with the voice of the morning alarm
I hear my child scream and shout
'Mom someone stole my attire'
I sneakily smiled to myself
And went back to my dream 'o' satire

– Fancy dress competition

He might be like a drop in the mighty ocean

Or be like the silent raindrops trickling down the stream.

He might be like thunder before the storm

Or be like the smooth sailing waves of a calm sea.

He might be like the furious rapids of the river

Or be the tornado himself.

Whatever be his nature,

He would always protect, secure and love his children.

For he is the essence of life like water

He is — the father

His form may change, but his purpose would always be the same

To support life

No matter we care, no matter we seek

He would always be there for us

In some form or another

– Fatherhood

Author Bio

Parul Kapoor was a creative by birth, yet her exploration of creative pursuits has been a meandering journey. After spending a considerable time on this planet, she discovered her true calling in poetry and writing. With its fluidity and potency, poetry soon became Parul's sanctuary, allowing her to navigate the labyrinth of her concealed sentiments, which often eluded expressions due to her introverted nature. Her debut poetry book titled '*Seeking identities*' is a collection of poems and verses, dedicated to all souls alike, who are continually in quest of their true identities, as she strongly believes humanity is not confined to singular identities but is a tapestry woven from myriad threads of experience. Through her poetic journey, she exposes the permanent scars and the healed wounds which have shaped the odyssey of her own transformation. When not penning poetry, Parul can be found working on her newsletter 'Blissed', published on Substack where she writes essays on slow & meaningful growth, relationships and urbanism. She also loves to immerse herself in the pages of non-fiction books or capture the sublime beauty of nature through her photographic lens. Her other interests include learning about different cultures through food, narratives, and soulful travel. Parul is a practicing urban planner and architect, who lives in Delhi with her family and her humble stack of books.

To explore more of Parul's work, follow her social media handles:

Website: https://linktr.ee/parulkapoor

Newsletter: https://parulkapoor.substack.com/

Instagram: https://www.instagram.com/
parulkapoor_unplugged/

LinkedIn: https://www.linkedin.com/in/parulkapoorunplugged/

www.ingramcontent.com/pod-product-compliance
Lightning Source LLC
Chambersburg PA
CBHW020500160726

47991CB00007B/2751

* 9 7 9 8 8 9 4 4 6 6 7 3 6 *